J

ALL AROUND THE WORLD
INDIA

by Joanne Mattern

pogo

Ideas for Parents and Teachers

Pogo Books let children practice reading informational text while introducing them to nonfiction features such as headings, labels, sidebars, maps, and diagrams, as well as a table of contents, glossary, and index.

Carefully leveled text with a strong photo match offers early fluent readers the support they need to succeed.

Before Reading

- "Walk" through the book and point out the various nonfiction features. Ask the student what purpose each feature serves.
- Look at the glossary together. Read and discuss the words.

Read the Book

- Have the child read the book independently.
- Invite him or her to list questions that arise from reading.

After Reading

- Discuss the child's questions. Talk about how he or she might find answers to those questions.
- Prompt the child to think more. Ask: How are the holidays that you celebrate different from those in India? How are they the same?

Pogo Books are published by Jump!
5357 Penn Avenue South
Minneapolis, MN 55419
www.jumplibrary.com

Library of Congress Cataloging-in-Publication Data

Names: Mattern, Joanne, 1963- author.
Title: India / by Joanne Mattern.
Description: Minneapolis, MN: Jump!, 2018.
Series: All around the world | "Pogo Books are published by Jump!" | Audience: Ages 7-10.
Includes bibliographical references and index.
Identifiers: LCCN 2017060849 (print)
LCCN 2017059272 (ebook)
ISBN 9781624969096 (ebook)
ISBN 9781624969072 (hardcover: alk. paper)
ISBN 9781624969089 (pbk.)
Subjects: LCSH: India–Juvenile literature.
Classification: LCC DS407 (print) | LCC DS407 .M352 2019 (ebook) | DDC 954–dc23
LC record available at https://lccn.loc.gov/2017060849

Editor: Kristine Spanier
Book Designer: Michelle Sonnek

Photo Credits: Alexandra Lande/Shutterstock, cover; Hemant/Adobe Stock, 1; Pixfiction/Shutterstock, 3; Jay Venkat/Shutterstock, 4 (foreground); Byelikova Oksana/Shutterstock, 4 (background); DR Travel Photo and Video/Shutterstock, 5; Sueddeutsche Zeitung Photo/Alamy, 6-7; Pavel Svoboda Photography/Shutterstock, 8-9; Bloomberg/Getty, 10; StanislauV/Shutterstock, 10-11; Dchauy/Shutterstock, 12; Frank Bienewald/imageBROKER/SuperStock, 13; Tier und Naturfotografie/SuperStock, 14tl; Kalakruthi/Shutterstock, 14tr; Prakash_Chandra/Shutterstock, 14bl; Sabi Locksmith/Shutterstock, 14br; imageBROKER/Alamy, 16-17; PhotosIndia.com LLC/Alamy, 18; powerofforever/Getty, 19; Vitaly Khodyrev/Shutterstock, 20-21; Deborah Lee Rossiter/Shutterstock, 23.

Printed in the United States of America at Corporate Graphics in North Mankato, Minnesota.

TABLE OF CONTENTS

CHAPTER 1

WELCOME TO INDIA!

Namaste! That is how you say "hello" in India. India is a large country in Asia. The incredible Taj Mahal is here.

India has beautiful mountains and vast farmlands. Let's explore this colorful country!

rickshaw

More than 1 billion people live in India. One third of India's people live in cities. The rest live in the country.

New Delhi is the country's **capital**. More than 18 million people live here. People get around on buses and trains. Some use **rickshaws**. Many work in factories. They make clothes and jewelry.

WHAT DO YOU THINK?

Why do you think rickshaws are a good way to get around busy streets in India?

About half of India's people work on farms. They raise sheep and goats. They grow rice and tea. Wheat. Cotton. Vegetables. Flavorful spices grow all over India as well.

DID YOU KNOW?

Europeans sailed to India in the late 1400s. They wanted the country's spices and gold.

tea ·····▶

Great Britain ruled India for almost 100 years. In 1947, India became an **independent** country. India has a **prime minister** and a president. The prime minister runs the country. The president represents the country at ceremonies and events.

Prime Minister Modi

TAKE A LOOK!

Each part of India's flag has meaning.

■ = courage and sacrifice
■ = truth
■ = faith and new life
■ = the wheel of life

CHAPTER 2

CLIMATE AND CREATURES

The Himalayas are mountains in northern India. They get a lot of rain and snow. The rest of the country is usually dry from October to May.

Monsoon season lasts from June to September. During this time, heavy rains fall across India. There are a lot of floods. The country depends on the water. **Crops** need it to grow. **Hydroelectric** power plants generate electricity.

elephant

tiger

monkey

peacock

The **climate** of India makes a comfortable home for animals. Large animals include water buffalo and elephants. Lions and tigers live in India, too. So do monkeys.

India is home to stunning birds. The peacock is the national bird. Parrots and cranes also live here.

Beautiful flowers grow in India. The lotus is India's national flower. It grows in water. Orchids, marigolds, and many other colorful plants grow here, too.

lotus

CHAPTER 3

INDIA'S PEOPLE

The people of India enjoy many festivals. **Diwali** is the festival of lights. People celebrate by lighting **diyas**. They also set off fireworks.

diya

Holi is the festival of colors. People throw colored powder and water on each other.

cricket

Cricket is a popular sport in India. It is similar to baseball. Soccer, golf, and **kabaddi** are also played here.

India is a unique country. Would you like to visit?

DID YOU KNOW?

India has the largest film industry in the world. More than 1,500 movies are made here each year!

QUICK FACTS & TOOLS

INDIA

Location: Asia

Size: 1.3 million square miles (3.3 million square kilometers)

Population: 1.3 billion (July 2017 estimate)

Capital: New Delhi

Type of Government: federal parliamentary republic

Languages: Hindi and English

Exports: clothing, petroleum, tea, rice, diamonds, chemicals

GLOSSARY

capital: A city where government leaders meet.

climate: The weather typical of a certain place over a long period of time.

cricket: A game played with a ball and bat.

crops: Plants grown for food.

Diwali: The Hindu festival of lights that celebrates happiness and wealth.

diyas: Oil lamps, usually made from clay, that are lit for Diwali.

Holi: A spring festival characterized by the throwing of colored water and powder.

hydroelectric: Using the power of water to produce electricity.

independent: Free from a controlling authority.

kabaddi: A game played between two teams in which the players take turns chasing members of the opposing team without being captured.

monsoon: A season or a storm that brings heavy rain.

prime minister: The leader of a country.

rickshaws: Three-wheeled vehicles that are either pedaled like a bike or have motors.

INDEX

TO LEARN MORE

Learning more is as easy as 1, 2, 3.

1) **Go to www.factsurfer.com**

2) **Enter "India" into the search box.**

3) **Click the "Surf" button to see a list of websites.**

With factsurfer, finding more information is just a click away.